For the Teacher

This reproducible study guide consists of instructional material to use in conjunction with a specific novel. Written in chapter-by-chapter format, the guide contains a synopsis, pre-reading activities, vocabulary and comprehension exercises, as well as extension activities to be used as follow-up to the novel.

NOVEL-TIES are either for whole class instruction using a single title or for group instruction where each group uses a different novel appropriate to its reading level. Depending upon the amount of time allotted to it in the classroom, each novel, with its guide and accompanying lessons, may be completed in two to four weeks.

The first step in using NOVEL-TIES is to distribute to each student a copy of the novel and a folder containing all of the duplicated worksheets. Begin instruction by selecting several pre-reading activities in order to set the stage for the reading ahead. Vocabulary exercises for each chapter always precede the reading so that new words will be reinforced in the context of the book. Use the questions on the chapter worksheets for class discussion or as written exercises.

The benefits of using NOVEL-TIES are numerous. Students read good literature in the original, rather than in abridged or edited form. The good reading habits formed by practice in focusing on interpretive comprehension and literary techniques will be transferred to the books students read independently. Passive readers become active, avid readers.

Novel-Ties are printed on recyled paper.

SYNOPSIS

Mark Brian, a young ordinand, is unaware that he has only a few years to live. Wanting the young man to learn as much as possible in the short time left, the Bishop sends him to the parish of Kingcome to live among the Kwakiutl, a band of native people living in the Pacific Northwest.

Mark's Kwakiutl deckhand, Jim Wallace, brings the ordinand to the ancient village. There Mark finds a dilapidated vicarage and inhabitants who are polite but remote, viewing the young ordinand with an air of "cautious waiting." Mark soon learns to care for the people in his charge, who include Chief Eddy; Peter, the carver; Mrs. Hudson, the matriarch who makes mashed turnips because the white man hates that vegetable; Marta Stephens, a genteel and kind woman with whom the Bishop has entrusted the secret about Mark's illness; Keetah, Mrs. Hudson's granddaughter; and Gordon, Keetah's betrothed, who longs to be part of the world outside the village.

As Mark struggles to adopt the lifestyle of the Kwakiutl, he participates in their loneliness and suffering, and comes to understand their constant frustration with the white man and with the loss of their young people to the outside world. Mark also takes part in their baptisms, their weddings, their burials, their fishing and hunting, and their celebratory potlatches. Unassuming and respectful, the ordinand begins to gain acceptance.

When Jim takes Mark to see the end of the salmon, called "the swimmer" by the Kwakiutl, Mark comforts a distraught Keetah by explaining the fish's death as natural and even a triumph. Mark's own demise is foreshadowed when he reveals he has a twin sister, thus making him one of the "salmon people." On the way back to the village, Jim discloses that Keetah will marry him because she and Gordon are not compatible. Although at this juncture Jim begins to take Mark into his confidence, it is on a hunting trip that their friendship is cemented by shared experience and mutual respect.

Sadness comes to the village when Keetah's sister plans to marry a white man, who tricks Gordon's uncle into selling him a valuable mask for only fifty dollars. After Keetah's sister and the man disappear, the elders of the family are so ashamed that they move to a deserted village. Later, Mark finds out that Keetah's sister was abandoned by the white man and died of a drug overdose.

Just before Gordon's mother dies in childbirth, Mark promises her to help Gordon get an education. The sadness of the funeral is relieved somewhat by the happy news that the elders of Keetah's family have returned from their exile. Chief Eddy comes with more good news: the Kwakiutl men have offered to help Mark build a new vicarage. This signifies that the cautious waiting is over, and Mark has been totally accepted by the Kwakiutl.

When Gordon returns from school in Vancouver, he behaves as though he has adopted the white culture and relinquished his Kwakiutl roots. His grandfather and uncle ask Mark to urge the boy to remain in the village, but the ordinand will not, feeling that Gordon must make his own decision. Gordon decides to remain in the outside world, and he takes Keetah with him. Mark hopes that if she decides to return to the village, she does so by choice and not by failure.

When Keetah does return, she avoids Mark at first, fearing his disapproval. She explains that she could not live in the outside world and that Gordon could not live anywhere else. She also discloses that she is going to have Gordon's baby, thus keeping a part of him in the village.

Seeing that Mark's physical condition is deteriorating, Marta writes to the Bishop, who comes to the village to inform Mark that he will soon be replaced. Considering all that has happened, Mark comes to the realization that he is dying. This is confirmed by Marta after he tells her that he heard the owl call his name.

The ordinand worries about returning to the white man's world to spend his final days, but the Kwakiutl confirm their love and acceptance of Mark by inviting him to stay with them until the end. While in their boat searching for a drunken logger, Mark asks Jim to treat Keetah well and to make sure that she is familiar with the outside world so she will be able to adapt when the village is no more. Soon after, lightning hits a tree, causing a slide that kills Mark. After the body is prepared for burial, Peter waits for the soul of the young vicar to return to the village he loved.

Note: Although "Native Americans" is the term currently used to refer to indigenous populations in North America, this book, published in 1973, refers to the Kwakiutl as "Indians." For the sake of consistency, this study guide is true to the book upon which it is based.

BACKGROUND INFORMATION

The Kwakiutl people live in Canada on the northern and eastern side of Vancouver Island as far south as Campbell River and on the mainland opposite. Their life is basically confined to a slender strip of coastal water, inlets, sounds, and hundreds of densely forested, almost impenetrable islands.

Although the Kwakiutl sometimes venture into the forest to collect wood or hunt, their lives have always centered on the sea, the waters of the northern Pacific Coast being one of the world's greatest fishing areas. The most important fish to these people has been the salmon, which live in the ocean but swim up rivers each year to spawn. The Kwakiutl fish on two types of boats – gill-netters and purse seiners. Gill netting is a one- or two-person operation, while seining requires a crew of four to seven.

The Kwakiutl built their villages in areas sheltered from fierce gales and high tides. A totem pole erected outside a house represents the status of the family living inside. These poles, which tell of important events in the mythic history of the family, are carved with crest symbols – images of humans, animals, and spirits who have a spiritual connection with the family. Besides totem poles, the Kwakiutl carve canoes, storage containers, weapons, and ceremonial items from red cedar wood.

The Kwakiutl society changed drastically after the first European traders arrived in the area in 1792. The introduction to white customs and beliefs caused conflict between those holding fast to tradition and those wanting to adopt new ways. The whites also brought strange new diseases that proved deadly for many who had no resistance to them.

Conditions worsened in the mid-1850's when the discovery of gold on Kwakiutl land brought many non-Indians to the area. The native peoples were driven off their land to make way for white settlers. Although the Kwakiutl continued to fish and hunt, they were now forced to earn wages, usually by working as fishermen or as employees in canneries. Anti-Indian laws passed in the late 1800's were enforced by government officials called agents, and missionaries arrived to convert the Kwakiutl to Christianity in the hope that they would abandon their native customs.

In spite of the best efforts of missionaries, the Kwakiutl held fast to their traditional rituals. The most important of these was a ceremonial feast called a *potlatch*, derived from the Nootka word *patshatl*, meaning gift. The potlatch, which has endured to this day, originated as the principal method of gaining status in Kwakiutl society. For each important family occasion, the host gives a potlatch, consisting of feasting, speechmaking, and dancing. Lavish gifts are presented to the guests to show true friendship and generosity. In giving a potlatch, the host hopes to elevate his own status by giving his guests more food and gifts than he has received at other potlatches. Reciprocation is expected, and thus gifts became the catalyst for fine craftsmanship among the Kwakiutl. In later years, however, the traditional gifts were supplanted by expensive, modern ones such as washing machines, causing families to become impoverished.

In 1884 the Canadian government passed a law prohibiting the potlatch ceremony. The Kwakiutl resisted the law and actually appear to have put on more and more lavish affairs during the late nineteenth and early twentieth centuries. After the prohibition was dropped in the 1950's, the Kwakiutl potlatch became public once again.

By the early 1960's many of the young among the Kwakiutl moved away from small, remote communities to inhabit one of four large villages: Alert Bay, Fort Rupert, Cape Mudge, and Kingcome Inlet. The Kwakiutl soon had support from the Canadian government to help them govern themselves and improve their own lives.

Today the Kwakiutl are organized into fourteen independent and self-governing bands, several of which have started their own school programs. Besides the customary subjects, these schools provide training in forestry, fishing, and carpentry. Children also learn traditional religious ceremonies from their elders. Potlatches and other traditional rituals have remained central to Kwakiutl life.

MINI-GLOSSARY

kwis-kwis	blue jay
Quee	name of the village (meanis inside place)
Whoop-Szo	noisy mountain
weesa-bedó	little boy
óolachon	candlefish
gleena	fish fat
che-kwa-á	fast moving water

PRE-READING ACTIVITIES

1. **Social Studies Connection:** Read the Background Information on pages two and three of this study guide and do some independent research on the Kwakiutl people. Focus on their history, occupations, family structure, myths, dances, crafts, and customs. In what ways is the Kwakiutl culture different from your own? In what ways is it similar?

2. Work with a cooperative learning group to locate photographs of Kwakiutl masks, carvings, and totem poles. What is the significance of each? What artifacts from other cultures would be analogous to these?

3. What is a "generation gap"? In what specific ways does your life differ from the lives of your parents as children. Has this caused any misunderstandings?

4. Folk tales and myths have always been part of oral tradition. They have played an important role in pre-scientific civilizations. Find an example of a "pourquoi" story, one in which a natural phenomenon is explained supernaturally. Why do you think this was done?

5. In every society there are celebrations marking the important events of birth, marriage, and death, as well as rites of passage. How do various religious and ethnic groups in our society commemorate these occasions? How have these traditions changed over the years?

6. Many ancient cultures are dying out because of contact with modern society. Do you think that people of these cultures should hold fast to the old ways or adapt to the outside world? Explain. Hold a class debate on this subject, using specific examples to support your point of view.

7. **Social Studies Connection:** Learn about the native peoples who inhabited your own area. Find out about their customs and lifestyle. Also, learn how they were affected by contact with white settlers, and whether their descendants still retain any of their original culture.

9. As you read the novel, use the map on page five of this study guide to trace the action. In what ways do you think that Kingcome's location affected the Kwakiutl culture there?

CANADA – Map of Kwakiutl Region

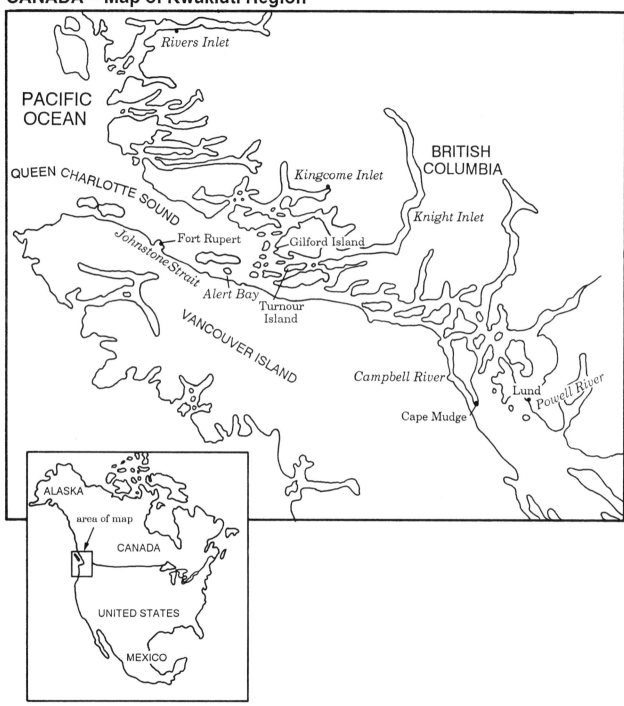

PART I — INTRODUCTION, CHAPTER I

Vocabulary: Draw a line from each word on the left to its definition on the right. Then use the numbered words to fill in the blanks in the sentences below.

1. ordinand   a. annoying

2. selvage   b. edge of woven fabric

3. exasperating   c. someone who functions as a priest or minister

4. garrulous   d. talkative

5. reminiscences   e. district with its own church (usually Roman Catholic or Anglican)

6. parish
                                                          f. recollections

. . . .

1. I complained to the usher about the _____ group of people sitting behind me at the movie theatre.

2. You do not need to hem the edge of the curtain because the _____ will not ravel.

3. The young _____ was nervous when he had to deliver a sermon to his new congregation.

4. People from the entire _____ assembled at church on Sunday morning to meet the new minister.

5. The old woman was full of _____ of her happy days as a young schoolteacher.

6. I found my friend's continual lateness _____.

Questions:

1. What must Mark face for which he is unprepared?
2. Why has the Bishop sent Mark to the village of Kingcome?
3. What is the English word for which there is none in Kwakwala?
4. As the story opens, what is the relationship between the young vicar and Jim Wallace?
5. Who are Caleb, Johnny Ray, and Calamity Bill?
6. What is the Kwakiutl name for the village of Kingcome? What does it mean?
7. What myths do the Kwakiutl relate to their village?

Part I — Introduction, Chapter 1 (cont.)

Questions for Discussion:

1. Why do you think the author has told us, even before we begin the book, that Mark is going to die?

2. How have the Kwakiutl learned to cope with the white man?

3. How have white people been insensitive to the Kwakiutl?

4. Why do you think the characters are not given names when they first appear?

5. What other creation myths are similar to those of the Kwakiutl?

Literary Elements: Exposition

Exposition is the part of a work of fiction in which the reader is given necessary background information. Record what you have learned about the setting, the characters, and the beginnings of a conflict in the chart below.

Setting	

Characters
  Mark
 	
  The Bishop
 	
  Caleb
 	
  Jim Wallace	

Conflict	

Part I — Introduction, Chapter 1 (cont.)

Literary Device: Simile

A simile is a comparison of two unlike objects using the words "like" or "as."
For example:

> He saw the small island, lovely as a jade jewel . . .

What is being compared?

_____

What is the effect of this comparison?

_____

Writing Activity:

Pretend you are Mark Brian. Write a journal entry describing your first impressions of Kingcome, the people, and the tasks that lie ahead. Be sure to include your feelings in your entry.

PART I — CHAPTERS 2, 3

Vocabulary: Use the context to determine the meaning of the underlined word in each sentence. Then find the exact meaning in a dictionary.

1. After proposing marriage, the man couldn't anticipate the woman's answer from her stolid expression.

   Your definition _____

   Dictionary definition _____

2. The minister held an open house at the vicarage immediately after church service.

   Your definition _____

   Dictionary definition _____

3. Her voice was tremulous with sobs.

   Your definition _____

   Dictionary definition _____

4. Since my friend moved out of state, we enjoy a weekly confabulation over the telephone.

   Your definition _____

   Dictionary definition _____

5. Because Mrs. Hudson was the matriarch, the other Kwakiutl woman would always defer to her judgment.

   Your definition _____

   Dictionary definition _____

6. When the wind howled and the temperature dropped below zero, he wore a toque to keep his head warm.

   Your definition _____

   Dictionary definition _____

Questions:

1. What difficult tasks does Mark face when he first enters the village?
2. Why hasn't the weesa-bedó been buried yet?
3. How does Constable Pearson reveal his insensitivity toward the Kwakiutl?
4. Why do the Kwakiutl remain at the gravesite after Mark has read from the Book of Common Prayer?

Part I — Chapters 2, 3 (cont.)

5. Why does Mark use the Victorian "we" among the Kwakiutl? What effect does it have upon them?

6. Who is Marta Stephens? What kind of favor does she bestow upon the Bishop who detests mashed turnips?

7. Do the Kwakiutl shoot deer? Explain.

8. How has Ellie's life been ruined? Why does she accept men who mistreat her?

Questions for Discussion:

What are your early impressions of Mark? Do you think he will eventually be accepted by the Kwakiutl?

Literary Element: Conflict

The plot of a novel is the arrangement of a series of incidents that make up the story. Conflicts – struggles between opposing forces – create the story's dramatic tension, moving the plot forward. There are several different kinds of conflict: conflict between people, conflict with society, conflict with nature, and personal conflict consisting of a mental struggle going on within a character. Describe the conflicts introduced so far. How do you think they might be resolved?

Literary Device: Foreshadowing

Foreshadowing refers to subtle clues an author gives to suggest what may happen later on in the novel. In this novel, we know what will happen, yet the author keeps referring to the subject of death. Look back over what you have read so far and list all the references to death you can find.

Writing Activity:

Mark must adjust to a new people and their culture. Think about a time when you had to adjust to a new situation, such as a move to a new neighborhood and school. Write about the problems you faced, how you overcame them, and your feelings throughout.

PART I — CHAPTERS 4, 5

Vocabulary: Word analogies are equations in which the first pair of words has the same relationship as the second pair of words. For example: LIFE is to DEATH as POLITE is to RUDE. Both pairs of words are opposites. Choose the best word from the Word Box to complete each of the analogies below.

```
                          WORD BOX

        stealthily       toll        fingerling
        spawn            amble        naiveté
```

1. STROLL is to _____ as CAUTIOUS is to CAREFUL.

2. _____ is to EXPERIENCE as GUEST is to HOST.

3. INTERVENE is to INTERFERE as BEGET is to _____.

4. SALMON is to _____ as DEER is to FAWN.

5. FIRMLY is to STAUNCHLY as _____ is to SECRETLY.

6. _____ is to BELL as SPLASH is to WATER.

Questions:

1. What hardships will Mark face along with the Kwakiutl?
2. What does Mark decide to do about the vicarage? What must he do first?
3. How does Mark help Sam and the teacher?
4. Why does Mark want to learn the Kwakiutl language?
5. During the first weeks, what are Mark's feelings about living in the Kwakiutl village?
6. What is the myth of the salmon and how is it related to Mark?
7. What does the author mean when she describes Gordon and Keetah as types of water? Why does this suggest that Keetah will marry Jim and not Gordon?

Part I — Chapters 4, 5 (cont.)

Questions for Discussion:

What causes the change in Mark's relationship with Jim? How do you know there is a change?

Literary Devices:

I. *Simile* — What is being compared in the following simile:

> We could see hundreds of silvery fish, moving secretly, almost stealthily, with a kind of desperate urgency, as an army moves to hold an outpost which must be reached at any cost.

_____

What is the effect of this comparison?

_____

Locate another example of a simile. Indicate page number, tell what is being compared and why the comparison has been made.

II. *Metaphor* — A metaphor is an implied comparison of two unlike objects in which no words of comparison are used. For example:

> There is a bear loose in the church.

What is being compared?

_____

Why do you think the author used this metaphor?

_____

Find two other metaphors in these chapters.

III. *Foreshadowing* — What further references to death or dying can you find?

_____

_____

Writing Activity:

Mark finds loneliness to be "an unavoidable element of life" in Kingcome. Write about a time when you felt loneliness. What caused your loneliness, and how did you overcome it? Compare your loneliness with that of Mark.

PART I — CHAPTERS 6, 7

Vocabulary: Synonyms are words with similar meanings. Draw a line from each word in column A to its synonym in column B. Then use the words in column A to fill in the blanks in the sentences below.

	A			B
1.	sustenance		a.	element
2.	suffice		b.	nourishment
3.	component		c.	lifeless
4.	horrific		d.	satisfy
5.	ravenously		e.	terrifying
6.	inanimate		f.	experimentally
7.	tentatively		g.	hungrily

. . . .

1. The angry driver shook his fist at the faulty traffic light even though he knew the _____ object could not respond.

2. A diet of bread and water has barely enough _____ to keep a person alive.

3. After a month of near-starvation, the released prisoner ate _____.

4. Hard work is always one _____ of success.

5. One microphone will not _____ to carry sound in the huge, new auditorium.

6. The little girl _____ tried to ride her bicycle without training wheels.

7. Sam let out some _____ moans when he caught his hand in the door.

Questions:

1. Why won't the Kwakiutl men talk about their hunting? What reason do they give Mark for the bear's death?

2. Why does Mark discontinue using the Victorian "we"?

3. What cements Jim and Mark's friendship?

4. By December, how is Mark's position in the village changed?

Part I — Chapters 6, 7 (cont.)

5. In his letter to the Bishop, what does Mark refute about the Indians' reputation?

6. What about the Christmas Eve service shows Mark how important the Kwakiutl have become to him?

Question for Discussion:

What is the significance of the statement, "Yes, my lord – no, my lord"?

Literary Devices:

I. *Personification* — Personification in literature is a device in which an author grants human qualities or actions to inanimate objects or abstract ideas. For example:

> He went to the door and opened it, and he stepped out into the soft white night, the snow whispering now under the footfalls.

What is the author personifying?

_____

How does this help you visualize the scene?

_____

_____

Use the device of personification to describe a scene that you know.

II. *Alliteration* — Alliteration is the repetition of the same initial letter, sound, or group of sounds in a series of words. For example:

> Have you had sufficient sustenance to suffice?

Why does the author use this device?

_____

_____

Find another example of alliteration in these chapters.

Writing Activity:

In Chapter Seven, Mark writes a letter to the Bishop. Only a few sentences of that letter appear in the book, however. Imagine you are Mark and complete the letter to the Bishop.

PART II — CHAPTERS 8, 9

Vocabulary: Use the context to help you choose the best meaning for the underlined word or words in each sentence. Circle the letter of the best answer.

1. Now for the first time the whole tribe was <u>in residence</u> and all the men were home from the fishing.

    a. on vacation   b. at home   c. asleep   d. fishing

2. The sound caught in the inlets, tossed from one steep mountain side to another, echoing and <u>reverberating</u>, and receding slowly to echo and re-echo far, far away.

    a. whispering   b. shouting   c. resounding   d. falling

3. . . . when this was done a <u>gale</u> was blowing, and it was too rough to return to Kingcome.

    a. strong wind   b. weak wind   c. snowstorm   d. bird

4. The guests were <u>billeted</u> in the houses of Kingcome, twenty or thirty to each house.

    a. found   b. clothed   c. fed   d. lodged

5. . . . in the old days the gifts had been so <u>lavish</u> they had beggared whole families and tribes and made others rich.

    a. extravagant   b. simple   c. complex   d. decorative

Questions:

1. What problems has the white people's schooling caused between the young and the old of the tribe?

2. What is the significance of Gordon's mask? Why doesn't Gordon's father sell it?

3. What problem does Mrs. Hudson foresee for Keetah's sister?

4. What meaning did the potlatches once have? Why did the government outlaw the great dance-potlatches? What remains of these celebrations?

5. How does the white man, who came with Keetah's sister, take advantage of Gordon's uncle?

6. Why does Keetah's family exile itself? What does this reveal about the moral standards of the Kwakiutl?

7. What question does Mrs. Hudson ask Mark out of sorrow? Why does Mark feel frustrated?

8. What is the Eskimo story that the Bishop wrote about to Mark? How does it relate to Mark's relationship with the Kwakiutl?

Part II — Chapters 8, 9 (cont.)

Questions for Discussion:

1. What is the significance of the title of Part II?
2. Who do you think is displaying greater bravery when Keetah and her sister part?
3. How are Mark and Gordon alike?
4. How can you explain the statement, "They were larger than themselves"?

Literary Devices:

I. *Anaphora* — Anaphora is a rhetorical device in which an author repeats an identical word or group of words in successive phrases, clauses, or verses. For example:

> The words lingered in the wind, in the spruce, in the drizzle that had begun to fall . . .

Why did the author choose to use anaphora?

_____

Find other examples and tell what effect they have.

II. *Irony* — Irony is an outcome of events opposite from what was expected by the characters or by the reader. In this novel what is the irony inherent in the young people's education?

_____

_____

What other ironies have the white man's influence on the Kwakiutl brought about?

III. *Symbolism* — A symbol in literature is a tangible object, person, or event that represents an idea or a set of ideas. What do the salmon symbolize to the Kwakiutl?

_____

What parallel exists between the salmon's lifelong quest and Mark's life?

_____

Writing Activity:

The reader does not know what is actually said between Keetah and her sister before the dance-potlatch. Write the dialogue that you imagine actually occurred between them.

PART II — CHAPTERS 10, 11

Vocabulary: Draw a line from each word on the left to its definition on the right. Then use the numbered words to fill in the blanks in the sentences below.

1. consent   a. without money

2. permeated   b. triumphantly, joyously

3. exultantly   c. spread, penetrated through

4. fronds   d. agreement

5. penniless   e. leaflike parts of a fern

. . . .

1. The fern _____ made a lacy pattern on the forest floor.

2. The smell of fresh coffee _____ the morning air.

3. They shouted _____ when they reached the top of the mountain.

4. Many families became _____ during the Great Depression.

5. Without the _____ of his parents he couldn't get a job.

Questions:

1. What is the óolachon and how is it celebrated?
2. Why does Mark wish to have Ellie sent away to school?
3. How does Keetah respond to Jim's discussion about marriage?
4. How does the news about Keetah's sister make Mark understand the source of the Kwakiutl's sadness?
5. What "gift" does the tribe offer to Mark? Why do they offer it at this time?

Question for Discussion:

Why do you think the author does not give Keetah's sister a name?

Writing Activity

In his letter the Bishop writes: "You suffered with them, and now you are theirs, and nothing will ever be the same again." Describe in your own words what he means by this statement.

PART III — CHAPTERS 12, 13

Vocabulary: Use a word from the Word Box to replace each underlined word or phrase in the following sentences. Write your choice on the line below the sentence.

```
              WORD BOX

    affable          ample
    boisterously     prefabricated
    prodigious       rebuked
              respite
```

1. The freight boat deposited the new <u>ready-made</u> vicarage on the float at the end of the inlet.

   _____

2. In order to transport the makings of the vicarage to the village, the men hired a forestry barge at an <u>outrageous</u> thirty dollars a day.

   _____

3. The gill-netters yelled loudly and <u>rowdily</u> for Mark and Jim to watch out for their nets.

   _____

4. After the vicarage was assembled, there was a brief <u>interval of rest</u> until the new furniture arrived and had to be carried upriver.

   _____

5. The people from the yacht were most <u>cordial</u>.

   _____

6. When Mark offered to help the English woman anthropologist, he was at once <u>criticized</u>.

   _____

7. Mrs. Hudson thought that T.P. Wallace would have <u>abundant</u> time on his five-hour trip to tell the anthropologist a long myth.

   _____

Part III — Chapters 12, 13 (cont.)

Questions:

1. How do Mark and the Bishop "cure" Mrs. Hudson when she feels she is going to die?
2. Why does the vicarage have to be finished by August?
3. Why does Mark encourage Keetah to write about the old ways?
4. What impact does the sale of liquor have upon the Kwakiutl in August?
5. What emergency arises on the Bishop's return trip? Why is Mark crying at the end?
6. Besides liquor, what other "friend" becomes an enemy in August? Explain.

Questions for Discussion:

How does liquor harm the village? How does Mark plan to deal with the people who had been humiliated? Do you think this is a reasonable solution?

Writing Activity:

Many visitors come to Kingcome village in this section of the book. Use a chart such as the one below to take notes about Chapters 12 and 13.

Guests	Behavior	Reaction of Villagers to Guests
Bishop		
Americans		
Anthropologist		

What conclusions have you reached? Explain them in a well-developed paragraph.

PART III — CHAPTERS 14 - 17

Vocabulary: Use words from the Word Box to complete the analogies below.

```
                        WORD BOX

        abashed    amenities        cormorants
        enmity     inert      macabre      slovenly
```

1. MISERLY is to GENEROUS as _____ is to TIDY.

2. PREJUDICE is to BIAS as MANNERS is to _____.

3. BIRDS is to _____ as DOGS is to POODLES.

4. _____ is to INACTIVE as INTRICATE is to ELABORATE.

5. HUMILITY is to EGOTISM as FRIENDSHIP is to _____.

6. _____ is to EMBARRASSED as DISTRESSED is to HARROWED.

7. AMUSING is to SATIRE as _____ is to HORROR STORIES.

Questions:

1. What do Mark and Jim have to teach the young boys before they leave the village for school?

2. Why are the old ones saddened by the departure of the young?

3. What surprise is waiting at the vicarage for Mark when he returns?

4. Why does Marta ask Mark to dinner the second night after he returns? How does he solve the problem presented to him?

5. What does Mark mean when he says that he came to know the Kwakiutl best through their loneliness?

6. On Christmas Eve, Gordon returns to the village a changed person. What choices will he have to make? Why doesn't Mark help him choose?

7. What decision does Gordon finally make? What is his rationale?

8. Why does Jim fear for Keetah when she decides to go with Gordon?

9. What is Caleb's prediction about the village?

Part III — Chapters 14 - 17 (cont.)

Questions for Discussion:

1. How are the young boys who are about to leave the village like Mark?

2. How does Mark realize how much he has changed? What doesn't he understand?

Literary Element: Characterization

In some ways Mark has changed from the time he first came to the village, and in other ways he has remained the same. Use the Venn diagram below to compare Mark as he was at the beginning of the novel with what he is like now. In what ways has he remained the same?

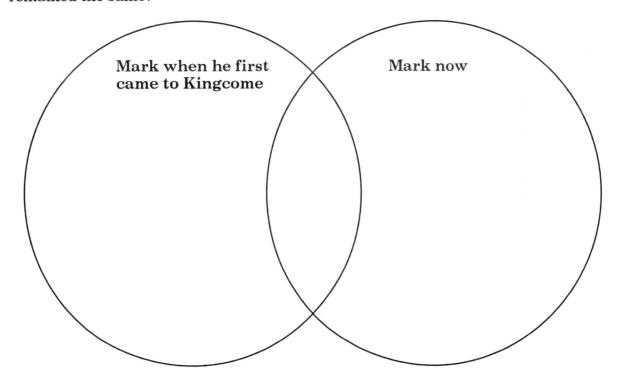

Writing Activity:

Many customs associated with death and burial have been discussed or alluded to in the novel. Select one of the following religions or choose one of your own to research. Write a paragraph discussing the customs of death in the religion you choose and compare them to those of the Kwakiutl.

- Ancient Egyptian
- Christian
- Buddhist
- Jewish
- Moslem
- Hindu

PART IV — CHAPTERS 18 - 20

Vocabulary: Antonyms are words with opposite meanings. Draw a line from each word in column A to its antonym in column B. Then use the words in column A to fill in the blanks in the sentences below.

A	B
1. leeward	a. proper
2. agnostic	b. guileless
3. unseemly	c. encouraged
4. squelched	d. fail
5. exodus	e. windward
6. unctuous	f. arrival
7. excel	g. believer

. . . .

1. Having always been good with figures, those students _____ in mathematics.

2. It is _____ for children to talk back to their parents.

3. To escape the fury of the gale, the captain steered his boat to a little cove on the _____ side of the island.

4. Because a fierce hurricane was approaching, there was a(n) _____ off the small island.

5. Wanting to set the record straight, the movie star _____ rumors that she would soon be getting a divorce.

6. The _____ saw little reason to attend church.

7. The convicted criminal's _____ manner fooled few people into believing his words.

Questions:

1. What problems face the villagers in January?

2. Why does the author use the metaphor that "the river was life itself . . ."?

3. How does Calamity face his coming death?

Part IV — Chapters 18 - 20 (cont.)

4. Why does Keetah return to the village? Why is she afraid to talk to Mark?
5. What indication do we have that Mark's physical condition is worsening?
6. What does the Bishop hint about during his talk with Mark on the boat?

Questions for Discussion:

1. How does the reason for Keetah's pregnancy clearly point up one difference between Indian and white man's culture?
2. What is the meaning of the title of the book?

Literary Device: Foreshadowing

How does Calamity's death foreshadow Mark's death?

_____

What does this event convey to Mark about the way one should meet death?

_____

_____

Writing Activity:

In these chapters, many contradictions become evident. In a well-written paragraph describe one of these contradictions. Then put yourself in the place of one of the characters and describe your feelings as you face this situation.

PART IV — CHAPTERS 21 - 23

Vocabulary: Draw a line from each word on the left to its definition on the right. Then use the numbered words to fill in the blanks in the sentences below.

1.	poignancy	a.	discerning
2.	staunch	b.	emotionally distressing quality
3.	contours	c.	outlines of figures
4.	resignation	d.	constant, faithful
5.	perceptive	e.	unresisting attitude
6.	efficacious	f.	rude
7.	inhospitable	g.	effective

. . . .

1. The athlete could accept the diagnosis of a broken bone with _____, knowing that he could try again for the Olympics in four more years.

2. At dusk it is difficult to see the _____ of a building in the distance.

3. It is _____ not to offer your guests anything to eat or drink.

4. Only a(n) _____ friend would walk you home on a cold, windy night.

5. This antibiotic is _____ in curing skin infections.

6. The tears on the mourners' faces attested to the _____ of the situation.

7. My _____ friend could tell that I was depressed even though I had a smile on my face.

Questions:

1. What are Mark's feelings as he contemplates his return to the world he had known before?

2. What does Mark understand when he hears the owl call his name? What is Marta's reply when Mark tells her that he has heard the owl?

3. What does Mark request of Jim concerning Keetah and why does he request this?

Part IV — Chapters 21 - 23 (cont.)

Questions for Discussion:

1. Has Mark achieved any form of success during his stay with the Kwakiutl? Explain.

2. Why do you think the author has Mark die after a rescue mission rather than due to his illness?

Literary Device: Symbolism

What does the river symbolize? Why is it appropriate that Mark die on the river?

_____

_____

What other symbols appear in the novel, and what do they symbolize?

_____

_____

_____

Writing Activities:

1. Write a letter from Mark to the new vicar of Kingcome.

2. Imagine that Mark left a letter to his Kwakiutl friends before his death. Write the letter he might have written. Be sure to mention specific people and refer to specific events.

CLOZE ACTIVITY

The following passage has been taken from Chapter 21 of the novel. Read it through completely and then fill in each blank with a word that makes sense. Afterwards, you may compare your language with that of the author.

How would he live again in the old world he had almost forgotten, where men throw up smoke screens between themselves and the fundamentals whose existence they fear but seldom admit? Here, where death waited behind each _____,[1] he had made friends with loneliness, _____[2] death and deprivation, and, solidly against _____[3] back had stood the wall of _____[4] faith.

How much had he accomplished? _____[5] he asked him, he knew what _____[6] Bishop's answer would be: "You may _____[7] know, or perhaps something you have _____[8] will reveal itself in Keetah's child, _____[9] Gordon's life. You have done your _____[10] bit."

And what had he learned? _____[11] not the truth of the Indian. _____[12] was no one truth. He had _____[13] a little of the truth of _____[14] tribe in one village. He had _____[15] the sadness, the richness, the tragic _____[16] of a way of life that _____[17] year, bit by bit, slipped beyond _____[18] and was gone. For a time he had been part of it, one of the small unknown men who take their stand in some remote place, and fight out their battle in a quiet way.

POST-READING DISCUSSION AND ACTIVITIES

1. Why do outsiders such as the teacher, the English anthropologist, and the tourists learn nothing of the Kwakiutl? In contrast, why is Mark able to learn so much about them?

2. Mark faces death several times among his friends: when he arrives, he must bury a weesa-bedó; later, he must deal with the death of Keetah's sister, Gordon's mother, and his friend Calamity. He also sees to the burial of ancestral bones. What does he learn from each of these experiences? In what way do they help him face his own mortality?

3. A theme is a central idea that is carried throughout a novel. Most novels have more than one central theme. Examine the following themes and discuss how each is manifest in the novel.

   - adapting to new circumstances
   - dealing with loneliness
   - death as part of the natural cycle of life

   - the importance of heritage
   - tradition versus change
   - the clash of different cultures

4. The point of view in a work of literature is the voice telling the story. This novel has a third person point of view, meaning that the author as an outside observer tells the story. When an author chooses to use one of the characters as the narrator, this is called a first person point of view. Why do you think that the author of *I Heard the Owl Call My Name* chose the third person point of view? Rewrite one of the chapters from the point of view of one of the characters. What impact does the change in point of view have on the story?

5. A myth is a story handed down through time which explains the unexplainable (i.e., season, creation, why the sun sets in the west). The Greeks, Romans, and Norsemen had gods and goddesses in their myths. Those of native people often involved nature. After having read many myths of the Kwakiutl in this novel, write your own myth explaining some natural phenomenon.

6. Write a short sequel to the novel, telling what happens to the main characters.

7. Obtain and view the film version of *I Heard the Owl Call My Name*. Compare the film with the novel. Do you think the movie remains true to the spirit of the book? Was the tragic plight of the Kwakiutl adequately portrayed? Were the characters appropriately cast? If you were the filmmaker, what would you have done differently?

8. Over a hundred years ago, anthropologist Franz Boas assumed the Kwakiutl to be a "dying culture." In fact, neither the Kwakiutl nor their traditions have died. What do you think acccounts for this longevity? What other cultures have endured over the years? What comparisons can you make between these cultures and that of the Kwakiutl?

SUGGESTIONS FOR FURTHER READING

* Achebe, Chinua. *Things Fall Apart.* Doubleday.

Benchley, Nathaniel. *Only Earth and Sky Last Forever.* Scholastic.

* Borland, Hal. *When the Legends Die.* Bantam.

Brown, Dee. *Bury My Heart at Wounded Knee.* Bantam.

Collier, Peter. *When Shall They Rest.* Dell.

Cooper, James Fenimore. *The Last of the Mohicans.* Bantam.

Forman, James. *People of the Dream.* Dell.

Gunther, John. *Death Be Not Proud.* HarperCollins.

Hale, Janet Campbell. *The Owl's Song.* Avon.

Highwater, Jamake. *Anpao.* HarperCollins.

Hudson, Jan. *Sweetgrass.* Scholastic.

Kroeber, Theodora. *Ishi, Last of His Tribe.* Bantam.

Lampman, Evelyn. *The Potlatch Family.* Macmillan.

* London, Jack. *Call of the Wild.* Penguin.

Neihardt, John C. *Black Elk Speaks.* Washington Square Press.

* O'Dell, Scott. *Sing Down the Moon.* Dell.

_____ *Zia.* Dell.

Paulsen, Gary. *Canyons.* Dell.

_____. *The Night the White Deer Died.* Dell.

* Richter, Conrad. *Light in the Forest.* Warner Books.

* Speare, Elizabeth. *Sign of the Beaver.* Dell.

Waters, Frank. *The Man Who Killed the Deer.* Pocket Books.

Other Books by Margaret Craven:

Again Calls the Owl. Dell.

The Home Front. Dell.

Walk Gently This Good Earth. Dell.

* NOVEL-TIES Study Guides are available for these titles.

ANSWER KEY

Introduction, Chapter 1

Vocabulary: 1. c 2. b 3. a 4. d 5. f 6. e; 1. garrulous 2. selvage 3. ordinand 4. parish 5. reminiscences 6. exasperating

Questions: 1. Mark is being moved by his bishop to a new parish where he will face a new life in an alien culture. 2. The Bishop has sent Mark to Kingcome village because he wants him to understand the meaning of life and that death is simply part of the natural cycle. 3. There is no word for "thank you" in Kwakwala. 4. Mark Brian and Jim Wallace have a very distant relationship. Mark is trying to be friendly, but Jim is shy and treats Mark with polite acceptance. 5. Caleb is an elderly priest who has worked successfully among the Kwakiutl. Johnny Ray is someone who died, whose spirit reputedly haunts the people. Calamity Bill is an eccentric hand-logger who lives in a shack. 6. Quee is the Kwakiutl name for the village of Kingcome. It means "inside place." 7. The myths the Kwakiutl believe are that their village was founded by one of two brothers who survived after the great flood and that long ago the gods turned a whale into a rock which they call "Whale Pass."

Chapters 2, 3

Vocabulary: 1. stolid – showing no emotion 2. vicarage – priest's or minister's residence 3. tremulous – shaky 4. confabulation – conversation 5. matriarch – woman who rules her family or tribe 6. toque – knitted wool hat

Questions: 1. When Mark first enters the village he has the difficult task of having to bury a little child. He must also unload the organ. 2. The body couldn't be buried without a government permit. The young government official waits for a temperate day to make his trip to the village and grant the permit. 3. Constable Pearson clearly has come to the burial only for the money, not for the love of the job or the people. 4. The Kwakiutl remain at the gravesite to perform their own ancient service. 5. Caleb advised Mark to use the Victorian "we," but it alienates the Kwakiutl. 6. Marta Stephens is a grandmother of the village. She gives the Bishop peas instead of turnips. 7. The Kwakiutl rarely shoot deer. Usually, they club them for food, not sport. 8. Ellie's life has been ruined because she has had sex with many men though she is only thirteen years old. She likes men who mistreat her because that is the only way she knows men: her father Sam treats her brutally.

Chapters 4, 5

Vocabulary: 1. amble 2. naiveté 3. spawn 4. fingerling 5. stealthily 6. toll

Questions: 1. Mark has to face life with inconveniences such as a house that is not weatherproof, wet wood to start a fire, poor plumbing, etc. 2. Mark decides to wait and then repair the vicarage. He must not ask for help but let the Kwakiutl offer to help him. 3. Mark turns down Sam when he begs for money. He suggests the teacher cut holes for his knees when he complains about his small bathroom. 4. Mark wants to learn the Kwakiutl language to gain a better understanding of the people and to be accepted by them. 5. During the first weeks he is there, Mark has a sense of futility and loneliness. 6. In ancient Kwakiutl myth it was believed that twins were not children at all, but really "swimmers," or salmon. Mark admits to being a twin and is thereafter associated with the salmon. 7. Gordon means "fast moving water," Keetah means "the pool." A pool is quiet and calm, while fast moving water always needs to move from place to place. Jim is a "pool" like Keetah.

Chapters 6, 7

Vocabulary: 1. b 2. d 3. a 4. e 5. g 6. c 7. f; 1. inanimate 2. sustenance 3. ravenously 4. component 5. suffice 6. tentatively 7. horrific

Questions: 1. The Kwakiutl men believe that if they talk about the hunt, the women will gossip, and the game will overhear and hide. They tell Mark the bear died because he was shocked to see a vicar on the mountain. 2. When Jim asks Mark if "we've" had enough," Mark realizes that this form of address is obsolete and inappropriate. 3. Jim and Mark's

friendship is cemented when it becomes clear that Mark can accept the Kwakiutl teasing and acknowledge their superiority in the ways of fishing and hunting. 4. Mark is now accepted by the Kwakiutl because they know he accepts them as they are. 5. Mark refutes the reputation that the Kwakiutl are simple, primitive, and emotional. 6. When the Kwakiutl come to him on Christmas Eve, he realizes that they are the "sheep of his pasture." He is responsible for their souls; they depend on him.

Chapters 8, 9

Vocabulary: 1. b 2. c 3. a 4. d 5. a
Questions: 1. Schooling has caused the young to adopt the customs of the white people, and the elders fear they will lose their Indian heritage. 2. Gordon has an ancient mask which contains his great-grandmother's hair. It has abalone eyes and is very valuable. Gordon's father doesn't sell it because it is used for the sacred dancing. 3. Mrs. Hudson realizes that Keetah's sister will not be accepted by the white man, and her village will be ashamed that she chose to leave them. 4. The potlatches were once the central purpose and ceremony of the Kwakiutl. They were outlawed because many families beggared themselves in their rivalries of generosity. They are now held rarely, on a small scale if at all. 5. The white man uses Keetah's sister to obtain the valuable mask which belonged to Gordon's uncle. 6. Keetah's family exiles itself because Keetah's sister shamed them. Answers to the second part of the question will vary. 7. Mrs. Hudson asks Mark, "What have you done to us?" Mark is frustrated because he knows that the Kwakiutl will have to change. 8. In the Eskimo story about Tagoona, the Bishop tries to assuage Mark's feeling of collective guilt for the white man. The Indian notion of man's problems on Earth is not the same as that of the white people.

Chapters 10, 11

Vocabulary: 1. d 2. c 3. b 4. e 5. a; 1. fronds 2. permeated 3. exultantly 4. penniless 5. consent
Questions: 1. The óolachon is the candlefish, and its arrival is celebrated with feasting. 2. Mark wants Ellie sent away because she is abused by her parents in the village. 3. Keetah says he has no manners. 4. Mark comes to realize how quickly the Indian can be perverted by the white man's way, and how deadly is the effect. 5. The tribe offers to help Mark build a new vicarage because he has suffered with them and has been accepted by them.

Chapters 12, 13

Vocabulary: 1. prefabricated 2. prodigious 3. boisterously 4. respite 5. affable 6. rebuked 7. ample
Questions: 1. Mark and the Bishop flatter Mrs. Hudson so that she feels well and can dance again. 2. The vicarage must be completed by August because heavy rains come in August, and the Indians can buy liquor then. 3. Mark fears the Kwakiutl will forget their old ways entirely. 4. In August, many Kwakiutl purchase alcohol and many become drunk and violent. 5. Dolores goes into labor sooner than expected. Mark cries because he is emotionally touched by the experience. 6. The river, usually an ally, becomes an enemy in August when it floods.

Chapters 14 - 17

Vocabulary: 1. slovenly 2. amenities 3. cormorants 4. inert 5. enmity 6. abashed 7. macabre
Questions: 1. Mark and Jim have to teach the boys manners and pride in their background. 2. The old ones know that the young will never again be part of the Kwakiutl culture in the same way. 3. When Mark returns, he finds the vicarage is clean and dusted and a loaf of fresh bread awaits him. 4. The old people want to talk to Mark about the deplorable state of their old burial ground. Mark decides to help them clear the area and place all of the old bones into a communal burial ground. 5. Mark is lonely, too. He thinks about the same things the Kwakiutl do because he has the same problems they have. 6. Gordon has to decide whether to remain in the village or go to school. Mark knows that the choice must be Gordon's. 7. Gordon decides to attend the University. He feels that he has changed too much to return to the old way of life. 8. Jim fears that Keetah will not be able to cope with life in the outside world. 9. Caleb predicts that the village will no longer exist.

Chapters 18 - 20

Vocabulary: 1. e 2. g 3. a 4. c 5. f 6. b 7. d; 1. excel 2. unseemly 3. leeward 4. exodus 5. squelched 6. agnostic 7. unctuous

Questions: 1. In January the villagers need to break the ice in the river to keep the boats moving. It is difficult to keep themselves warm and alive. 2. The river provides transportation, is their link with the outside world; the fish they need for survival come from the river. 3. Calamity accepts death with candor and a sense of humor. 4. Keetah returns to the village because she cannot feel at home in the white man's world. She fears that Mark will not approve of her pregnancy. 5. Marta notes Mark's physical condition is worsening when he appears particularly pale and wan. She sees the look of approaching death on his face. 6. The Bishop mentions that he will be sending a replacement for Mark. This suggests that he realizes Mark has come to the end of his life.

Chapters 21 - 23

Vocabulary: 1. b 2. d 3. c 4. e 5. a 6. g 7. f; 1. resignation 2. contours 3. inhospitable 4. staunch 5. efficacious 6. poignancy 7. perceptive

Questions: 1. Mark is sad and fearful as he contemplates his return to the white man's world. 2. Mark understands that the weakness he had felt means impending death. Marta agrees with his interpretation. 3. Mark wants Jim to treat Keetah as a white man treats his wife so that she will eventually feel comfortable when she is forced to leave the village with all of the others.